THE KEEFER
ROULETTE SYSTEM

HOW TO MAKE
$1,000
PER DAY PLAYING ROULETTE

JEREMY B KEEFER

Order this book online at www.trafford.com
or email orders@trafford.com

Most Trafford titles are also available at major online book retailers.

Printed in the United States of America.

ISBN: 978-1-4907-5452-9 (sc)
978-1-4907-5453-6 (e)

Our mission is to efficiently provide the world's finest, most comprehensive book publishing service, enabling every author to experience
success. To find out how to publish your book, your way, and have it available worldwide, visit us online at www.trafford.com

Trafford rev. 01/31/2015

Trafford
PUBLISHING®   www.trafford.com
North America & international
toll-free: 1 888 232 4444 (USA & Canada)
fax: 812 355 4082

CONTENTS

INTRODUCTION

Typically, gambling propositions offer negative cash flow, but I have done considerable research and have combined my knowledge of mathematics and probability with the game of roulette to create a wealth-generating system! Rather than keep this knowledge to myself, I want to offer you a chance to also create a better lifestyle for you and your family. In today's marketplace, it is difficult to confidently hand over your hard-earned money to others and have them grow it for you. Stock price manipulation, Ponzi schemes, declining markets, and global uncertainty make it scary to entrust your funds to other investors. Do you really have control of how your funds are being invested? I believe the best person to trust in handling your financial future should be yourself! This book and my system will start you on that path to financial freedom.

With my unique betting system—the Keefer Roulette System (or Keefer Betting System, as it can be utilized in other mediums)—an investor or gambler can control how much of his funds are being invested, when they are being invested, and when they are withdrawn. It gives the user total control; and the best part is that it's fun, unlike spending countless hours researching boring stocks or mutual funds. This book is like a map, leading you to financial freedom. In it, I will teach you my system step-by-step. You can then use my method to start making a lot of money and start living your life the way you've always wanted!

There are two ways to enhance the financial status of your life—you can continue to earn the same amount and spend less OR you can earn more money. Of course, most people would agree that earning more money is the best way to accomplish financial freedom, but most people do not have a means of increasing their annual income. The system I have devised has helped me to earn more money, thus allowing me to save much more after paying my monthly bills. My system can also help you to make as much extra money as you'd like. Just putting in a half-day per week can generate over $15,000 per year in extra income. Would an extra $15,000 help you pay your bills each month, settle debts, take vacations, or save for retirement? Of course, the more time you devote to this system, the more money you can make! Some two-man teams using my system will play four or five days per week and make in excess of $150,000 per year! Your schedule and financial goals will determine how much money you make with the Keefer Roulette System. Thanks for taking an interest in my system and good luck in your endeavors!

Jeremy B. Keefer

CHAPTER 1

ROULETTE GAMEPLAY, BETS, AND PAYOUTS

Roulette is a game that is found at almost every casino. First appearing in Europe a few hundred years ago, the game really hasn't changed much since its inception. The gameplay includes a spinning wheel with either 37 or 38 numbers, a corresponding tabletop with the same numbers, and a ball. Players have the opportunity to bet which number will be spun and place wagers on these numbers. Once wagers are set, the dealer spins the ball around the roulette wheel and the number it lands on is the winning number. Essentially half of the numbers on the wheel are Even and half are Odd. Each number is assigned a color (either Red or Black). Players can also bet on these outcomes. Due to the various possible bets, people have many betting strategies for roulette.

When the game of roulette was invented, the wheel contained the numbers 1-36 and the number "0". Once the game migrated to North America, another number, "00", was added to the wheel. This additional number slightly alters the probabilities and gives the house (or casino) a slightly higher edge. In Europe, establishments continue to use the single-Zero wheel so that type is typically called European Roulette, while the tables with a "0" and "00" are referred to as American Roulette. The following picture shows the two wheels.

European Wheel

American Wheel

To demonstrate how this additional number affects the probabilities, let's look at the math below:

On a European Roulette wheel, there are 18 Red numbers, 18 Black numbers, and 1 Green number. Out of these same slots, there are 18 Even numbers, 18 Odd numbers, and 1 Zero (neither Even nor Odd).

If you were to bet on Even, Odd, Red, Black, 1-18, or 19-36, your chance of winning your wager is 18 out of 37 possible outcomes. This ratio (18/37) translates to a 48.65% chance of winning your bet. On these bets, you will be paid 1:1 on your bet, so if you bet $20 that the next number will be Black and it lands on a Black number, you will win $20. The house will make money in the long-run on these bets because you always have a 48.65% chance of winning and a 51.35% chance of losing.

On an American Roulette wheel, there are 18 Red numbers, 18 Black numbers, and 2 Green numbers. Out of these same slots, there are also 18 Even numbers, 18 Odd numbers, and 2 Zeroes (0 and 00—neither Even nor Odd).

If you were to bet on Even, Odd, Red, Black, 1-18, or 19-36, your chance of winning your wager on an American wheel is 18 out of 38 possible outcomes. This ratio (18/38) translates to a 47.37% chance of winning your bet. As you can see, on an American Roulette wheel, you lose over 1.2% more of your bets than on a European wheel due to that additional "00".

Players can also select any of the numbers on the wheel to bet on. For example, imagine you bet $5 that 17 will be spun. 17 hits. You will be paid 35:1 for this win, or $175 for your $5 bet. On these bets, the house edge is even greater as your probability of hitting a specific number is 37:1 on a European wheel or 38:1 on an American wheel, but the payout is only 35:1. If you bet $5 on the same number 38 times, theoretically you will only hit it once. Over those 38 spins, you will lose $185 (37 losses) and win $175 (on the winning spin), therefore losing $10 overall. Losing $10 out of $190 total bets means the house has a 5.26% edge.

Of course theoretical probability doesn't always hold true in roulette. Although we can accurately calculate theoretical odds for any situation in roulette, we typically see short-term trends or streaks. Most roulette tables today feature a digital board displaying the last 15-25 results. Often, you will find the same number more than once on that board. Some people are convinced they can spot various trends on each roulette wheel; sometimes, depending on the grooves worn in the wheel from thousands of spins, the way a particular dealer spins the ball, or some other factor, a wheel can produce the same number several times over a short period.

Let's take a look at the betting area of a roulette table and discuss the various bets available. The image below shows the betting area of an American Roulette table.

Players can wager several bets on each spin. "Inside bets" are bets made on specific numbers. Any of the Black or Red numbers from 1-36 and the two Green numbers (0 and 00) can be bet individually. The payout when a player chooses the correct individual number is 35:1. The theoretical odds of winning this bet is 1 in 38 as you have 1 possible winning outcome and 37 possible losing outcomes. Other inside bets include Street bets, Corner bets, etc. These bets allow the player to bet on neighboring numbers, such as 1 and 2 or 16, 17, 19, and 20. The Keefer Roulette System does not use inside bets.

Players can also make "outside bets," called so because their respective boxes are outside the board of numbers. When a player bets on First, Second, or Third 12, he is hoping that the winning number is in that group of 12 numbers. First 12 refers to numbers 1-12, Second 12 refers to numbers 13-24, and Third 12 refers to numbers 25-36. The payout when a player chooses the correct group of 12 is 2:1 or double your money. The theoretical odds of winning this bet is 12 in 38 as you have 12 possible winning outcomes and 26 possible losing outcomes. The Keefer Roulette System does not use these bets.

Players can also make a similar bet, betting on each column. These bets are on the right side of the image and are marked "2 to 1". Each box represents the column next to it. For example, if you bet on column 1, you are betting that the next spin will land on 1, 4, 7, 10, 13, 16, 19, 22, 25, 28, 31, or 34. If it does, you are paid 2:1. Once again, you have a 12/38 or 31.58% of winning. The Keefer Roulette System does not use these bets either.

The betting boxes at the bottom of the table (1-18, Even, Red, Black, Odd, and 19-36) are the only bets you will ever use when using my system. The principal reason is that while only paying out even money to your bet or 1:1, you have the greatest probability of winning your bet. With each of these bets, you have 18 possible winning outcomes and 20 possible losing outcomes, giving yourself a 47.37% probability of winning on each spin. This is critical to the Keefer System as we will discuss in Chapter 3. As you can see, the house still maintains a small edge on these bets due to the 0 and 00. In other words, if the two Zeroes were not on the board, betting on either of these boxes (1-18, Even, Black, Red, Odd, or 19-36) would all have a 50/50 chance of winning on any given spin. The Keefer Roulette System will allow you to overcome this house edge and will in fact give you a statistical, mathematic advantage over the long-run.

CHAPTER 2

OTHER SYSTEMS AND WHY THEY DON'T WORK

Over the years, many people have attempted to devise betting strategies to overcome the house edge in roulette. I have done a lot of research on the Internet about these strategies, and through several trial runs, have discovered that none of them work consistently. The Keefer Roulette System does however use some basics from one of the first and most widely used roulette betting systems—the Martingale System.

The Martingale System is believed to have originated in the 1700s in France. With this system, a gambler would make a wager on a 50/50 chance (or something close to that). If he won the bet, he saw a profit. If he lost the bet, however, he would double his previous bet until finally winning, thus erasing all previous losing bets.[1] For example, if a player bet $5 on Even (47.37% on an American roulette table and 48.65% on a European table), and lost his initial bet, he would bet $10 on the next spin. If he lost the second spin, he would bet $20—or double the previous bet. If the third spin was Odd again, he would continue to bet $40 and so on until an Even number was spun. Because the player doubles his bet each time, once he finally hits that Even number, that one win will cover each previous loss plus a profit of one unit. In the example above, if it takes five spins to hit an Even number, the player would have bet the following amounts: $5, $10, $20, $40, and $80 respectively for a total of $155. The first four bets he lost totaled $75, so when he is paid 1:1 on his $80 bet, the $75 lost in the previous four spins is recovered plus a profit of $5.

As you can see, this system does offer a lot of promise. However, there are some drawbacks to the Martingale System. Firstly, the player needs a very large bankroll to cover prolonged losing streaks. If he loses eight consecutive bets, he will have to bet $1,280 on the ninth spin just to make a $5 profit. I have seen times where the ball lands on Red numbers nine straight times or Even numbers eight straight times. *It can and does happen from time to time.*

Even if the player does have a very large bankroll, casinos are prepared to deal with Martingale bettors. The way the house deals with these bettors is by establishing table limits on each table. For instance, a roulette table at your local casino may have a $5 minimum bet and $1,000 maximum bet. These limits are not random. Casinos know that many people will use this betting system and consequently predetermine table limits to flaw the system. At a $5/$1,000 limit table, a player could only lose eight consecutive bets before reaching the table max. Once the table maximum is reached, the player has already lost hundreds of dollars but is unable to bet enough on the ninth spin to recover all losses.

Since the 1700s, several attempts have been made to slightly alter the Martingale System to make it more effective. The first variation we will discuss is the Reverse Martingale Strategy. This strategy works the same way, but the bets are only doubled each time a player wins a bet and dropped back to the initial unit bet once the player loses a spin. Let's say a player bets $5 on Red and it comes Red—the player wins $5. On the next spin, he bets $10 on Red and it comes Red again. Now he has won $10. On the third spin he bets $20 on Red; it comes Black. Now the player has lost $20, which is more than the $15 he won on the prior two spins. As you can see, this system will only work short-term when the bettor goes on a lucky streak and as soon as that streak ends, he will be left with no profit unless he cashes out or decreases his bet before it ends. This is a system you should never use.

Another variation worth noting is the Grand Martingale System. This system states that when a losing bet occurs, the player must then double the bet and add another amount to each bet. For example, if the bettor loses $5 on the first spin, he must bet $11 (double the $5 plus $1) on the second spin. If he loses that, he must then bet $23 (double the $11 bet plus $1) on the third spin. This system only increases your winnings very slightly on winning sessions, but also increases your bet sizes more quickly on losing sessions, giving you less chances of winning and maximizing your losses. Once again, this system decreases your chances of success.[2]

There are several other "systems" out there found on websites and video sites today. Although they may seem to give you an edge over the house, I have yet to see one other system that accomplishes this based on actual mathematics and probability. I think you will find that the Keefer Roulette System is the only system that allows the bettor to stay within the table limits while still allowing him a very high probability of profiting each session.

CHAPTER 3

THE "KEEFER ROULETTE SYSTEM"

The Origin

As a senior in high school, I joined a group of friends in learning how to play Texas Hold'em poker. It quickly became our favorite thing to do as we would meet once or twice per week and play for our share of $25. Of course, in high school, that seemed like a lot of money to earn while playing a game. Over the next few years, we would all work on the game, trying to understand its ins-and-outs. At first, I was losing more than I was winning; then I started reading about percentages, pot odds, implied odds, and equity and slowly started to improve. Using mathematics, probability, and other cognitive skills to earn money at poker was an exhilarating challenge!

For many, games like poker are what I call 'gateway games.' When I turned 21, the only game I knew how to play was Texas Hold'em—then I went to Atlantic City for the first time with my good friend Tony. My first walk through one of the large casinos opened my eyes to the multitude of games and exciting action offered on the gaming floor. Although I only focused on playing poker my first several trips to A.C., an interest to learn the other games was developing. Over time, I have learned how to play Blackjack, Craps, Roulette, 3- and 4-Card Poker, Baccarat, and others. A few of these games became a small hobby whenever I had a few extra dollars to spend.

However, these games are all tilted in favor of "the house," or casino. In fact, you may have even heard the phrase, "the house always wins," a common phrase of the industry. Basically, it means that in all games spread across the gaming floor, the casino has at least a slightly higher percentage of winning, and therefore, they will make money off each guest in the long-run.

As a long-time student of mathematics and probability theory, I felt a strong desire to see if I could come up with a method of lowering the house's edge. Through extensive research and trials, most systems I tried were not effective enough. At a point where most people would have simply given up, I did some experiments with betting strategy. It was here that I discovered what I thought could be the answer.

Once I had this new idea, I met with my good friend Brandon DeLaney and ran my thoughts by him. Brandon has always been one of my smartest colleagues and he also has a knowledge of the various games. Upon hearing about my system, he made a couple suggestions that helped to shape the end result. He suggested that I focus solely on roulette, rather than other games, as roulette is more random than card-based table games. He was right about that as the system I was developing relied heavily on randomness. Rather than adapting a system that could apply to multiple games, I focused it solely on roulette.

After tuning my system's theory slightly, Brandon also helped me to run some initial trials before putting it into practice on a live roulette table. His insights have been invaluable to the origins of the Keefer Roulette System.

The Strategy Explained

The Keefer Roulette System is comprised of a few simple components that anyone can follow to make a substantial return.

- This system works best with a two-person team; while one player can achieve success, delegating the bets to two players not only simplifies the betting process, but it also reduces each person's investment risk by 50%

- The two players bet against each other – prior to starting a new session, the team must determine which of the three betting options they will use; a team can bet on Black and Red, Even and Odd, or 1-18 and 19-36; these are the only bets used by the Keefer Roulette System; if the Black/Red option is chosen, player 1 will only place bets on Black and player 2 will only place bets on Red; if the Even/Odd option is chosen, player 1 will only bet on Even and player 2 will only bet on Odd; if the 1-18/19-36 option is chosen, player 1 will only bet on 1-18 and player 2 will only bet on 19-36

- Once each player knows what his bet will be each spin, he simply follows a strict betting pattern until the end of the session; each player starts the betting at one unit; he will continue to bet one unit until his first losing bet, after which his bet size will increase to two units; if he loses two consecutive bets, he increases his third bet to three units; if he loses three or more consecutive bets, he must double the size of his previous bet until he wins a bet; whenever his bet is a winner, he must immediately reduce his subsequent bet to one unit on the next spin and the process is restarted

- Only one bet is placed at the beginning of each session and this bet remains until it loses the first time; once the first bet does lose, both players bet on each spin until the end of the session; example: player 1 will start the session by betting on Even; he will continue to bet one unit on Even for each spin until Odd or Zero is spun (and he loses his bet); once he encounters his first loss, he ups his Even bet to two units and player 2 starts on Odd with one unit; at this point, each player follows the betting pattern described above, raising his individual bet after each loss and lowering his bet back to one unit after each win

- While wagering opposite bets, the players will NEVER bet the same amount – if player 1 wins a bet, he drops down to one unit on the next spin; simultaneously, if player 1 wins on a spin, player 2 will lose on that same spin so he will be required to up his bet on the next spin

- If a Zero or Double-Zero occurs, both players must increase their next bets according to the betting pattern

- The typical arrangement for partners in this investment requires both players to bring the same amount to the table (enough to cover eight straight losses depending on the table stakes); once the money is brought to the table, it is essentially viewed as a 50/50 venture; therefore, if one player makes a profit of $200 and his partner makes a profit of $100, each player will take home a profit of $150; additionally, any funds at the table must be used to adhere to the Keefer Roulette System betting pattern for optimal success

- Each player must bring enough chips to cover eight consecutive losses; for example, at a $5 minimum/$1,000 maximum table, each player must bring $960; when starting with a $5 bet, $960 will cover eight consecutive losses ($5 + $10 + $15 + $30 + $60 + $120 + $240 + $480 = $960); after eight consecutive losses, one player may be out of funds, but as this is a joint venture, the other player will have enough to cover the ninth bet; if the board comes Odd eight straight spins, the player betting on Odd may not have enough accumulated profit to cover the ninth bet, so his teammate will use his funds to cover the $960 Odd bet for the ninth spin

- THE ONLY WAY THE TEAM WILL LOSE MONEY WITH THIS SYSTEM IS IF ONE OF THE PLAYERS LOSES NINE CONSECUTIVE BETS. As long as both players continue to win at least one of every eight bets, the team will consistently and systematically earn a profit; when a player does lose nine in a row, he typically reaches the table maximum bet and cannot proceed; I call this occurrence the "Streak of 9" and once this happens, the session is over

The chart below displays the Even/Odd bets of each player for the first ten spins of a new session. Hopefully this chart will clarify any questions you may have about the betting strategy of the Keefer Roulette System.

Betting Chart-Start of New Session			
Spin	Player 1's Bet (Even)	Player 2's Bet (Odd)	Outcome
1	$5	-	Even
2	$5	-	Odd
3	$10	$5	Odd
4	$15	$5	Even
5	$5	$10	Even
6	$5	$15	Even
7	$5	$30	Even
8	$5	$60	Odd
9	$10	$5	Even
10	$5	$10	Odd

Let's look at an explanation of the bets in the chart above. To start the session, the team decided to bet on Even. Choosing only one bet for the start of the session helps in two ways:

1. If both players started at one unit on the first spin, the team already cannot make a profit on that spin because when one player wins, the other player loses the same amount. However, if a Zero is spun, both players will lose and both will have to increase their bets to two units.

2. If, by chance, the session starts with a Streak of 9, and the team happens to select the right starting bet, it avoids a losing session. For example, if a team decides to bet on Black and Red, and they choose to start the betting with Black, they will avoid a losing session if the first nine numbers are any combination of Blacks and Zeros (as a Red bet will lose those nine spins).

In the chart above, the players elect to start with Even—and an Even number was spun so the team earned $5. As player 1 did not yet lose his initial bet, he will bet $5 again on Even—and an Odd number came. As a result, player 1 lost his $5 bet and must bet $10 on Even for the next spin. Additionally, since player 1 lost, player 2 will start betting on Odd (one unit). With $10 on Even and $5 on Odd, the third spin produced another Odd number. Player 1 loses his $10 bet and player 2 wins $5. Player 1 must increase his bet to $15 (3 units) as he just lost two straight and player 2 keeps his bet at $5 as he just won the last spin.

Spin 4 resulted in an Even number, winning $15 for the team while their $5 Odd bet lost. For the next spin, player 1 will revert to a $5 bet as he won and player 2 must up his bet to $10 as he lost. That's all there is to the Keefer Roulette System! Just place a bet on one box; if it wins, collect your winnings and reduce your bet to one unit; if it loses, increase your bet according to the betting chart!

This betting system that I have devised is similar to the Martingale Betting System, with one little twist. As we discussed in Chapter 2, the Martingale System requires a bettor to double his bet after each loss. The one change I made to that betting pattern is to *double* the bet after the first loss, and after the second straight loss a player will *add one unit* rather than doubling the previous bet. All bets after this are then doubled. What does this one small change accomplish? With the Keefer System, we sacrifice any profit after losing two consecutive bets and only break even once a player does win. With the Martingale System, a player will make a one-unit profit whenever the player finally wins a bet. Still, remember that the Keefer System is based on two players betting opposites, so while one player may break even over six or seven spins, his partner is earning them a profit over that same span. The Martingale System does not rely on players betting against each other, so following that betting system will only produce a $5 profit over the course of those six or seven spins while the Keefer System may produce a $25-35 profit.

The other critical advantage that this change provides is the fact that players can have a longer losing streak and still come out on top. Decreasing the third bet from four units to three allows all subsequent losing bets to be exponentially lower with the Keefer System, thus giving you more opportunities to win before reaching the table maximum. Keep in mind that table maximum amounts are consciously determined by casinos to prevent people from being successful with strategies like the Martingale System. If there was no table limit and a player had a virtually unlimited source of funds, he could keep doubling his bet over and over until he finally won all his money back. As this is not a reality, I had to design a strategy that could work a very high percentage of the time while staying within these very real parameters. The chart below shows how this key difference affects subsequent bets at a table with a $5 minimum bet and $1,000 maximum bet.

Martingale System v. Keefer System				
Bet		Martingale System		Keefer System
1		$5		$5
2		$10		$10
3		$20		$15
4		$40		$30
5		$80		$60
6		$160		$120
7		$320		$240
8		$640		$480
9		Table Max Reached		$960

Note: As you can see from the chart above, changing the 3rd bet from $20 (double the previous losing bet) to $15 (which only covers the previous two losing bets) allows each subsequent bet to be lower, which also allows the player to have one more opportunity to win his money back. With the Martingale System, the player will make a $5 profit whenever he finally wins a bet. With the Keefer System, the player will make a $5 profit as long as his bet hits on the first or second spin. Every spin afterward will award the bettor with $0 profit, but also $0 lost. The benefit of the Keefer System is that, while sacrificing that $5 profit from spins 3-9, he has an extra spin, or an extra 47.37% chance to recover his losses. Each player's responsibility to the team is to simply follow the Keefer System betting structure.

The Mathematics Behind the System

Actual mathematics based on theoretical probability are the only way to quantify the success of the Keefer Roulette System. Casinos use this same method to determine table stakes, payout odds, etc. to ensure they will turn a profit over the long-run. The remainder of this chapter is all about the mathematics behind the system, showing exactly how you finally have an edge over the house!

The most important calculation of the Keefer Roulette System is the odds of having a losing session. Remember, the only way for a team to lose money is to have a Streak of 9, or a nine-spin streak where one of the two players loses each spin. As you can imagine, when a player is always betting on a chance that is almost 50/50, it is very unlikely he will lose that bet nine consecutive times. It does happen however, and here are the odds:

When betting on one of the permitted parameters of this System (Even, Odd, Black, Red, 1-18, or 19-36), there are 20 potential losing outcomes out of 38 possible outcomes (1-36, 0, and 00). In other words, if you were to bet on Black, there are 20 numbers that are either Red or Zero, thus there are 20 numbers that will lose your bet. This equates to a 52.63% of losing your bet on the first spin.

Your chances of losing the same bet twice in a row is considerably lower, but still too prevalent. To calculate the odds of this, we take the percentage of losing the first spin and multiply it by itself: .5263 x .5263 = .2770 or 27.70%. This means if you were to bet on Black on two consecutive spins, you should lose both spins about 1 out of 4 times.

Your chances of losing the same bet three times in a row are .5263 x .5263 x .5263 = 14.58%

Your chances of losing the same bet four times in a row are .5263 x .5263 x .5263 x .5263 = 7.67%

This pattern continues to infinity. As you can see, your odds of losing a near-50/50 bet four straight times are much lower than losing that same bet once or twice. A great way to think of it would be flipping a standard coin. If you were to bet "heads" on the flip of a coin every time, you would have a 50/50 chance of winning on the first flip. However your chances of it being tails the first two times is less than 50%. Your chances of it being tails five, or six, or seven straight times is even more unlikely. The same principle applies to the Keefer Roulette System and that is exactly why we only bet on either Even and Odd, Black and Red, or 1-18 and 19-36—they are similar to flipping a coin!

This chart will show you the percentages of losing consecutive spins on a random wheel:

# Spins Lost (Consecutive)	% of Losing (American)	% of Lowing (European)
1	52.63%	51.35%
2	27.70%	26.37%
3	14.58%	13.54%
4	7.67%	6.95%
5	4.04%	3.57%
6	2.13%	1.83%
7	1.12%	0.94%
8	0.59%	0.48%
9	0.31%	0.25%

This chart is a great way to see how the additional "00" affects your odds in American Roulette. It also shows that, by following my System, you and your partner will only have a .31%, or 31 out of 1,000 chance of losing money. Since you will lose more on losing sessions than you will typically earn in winning sessions, we must also calculate our expected profit with this in mind.

100% of results / .31% chance of losing nine consecutive spins = 322.58

This means that out of 322 nine-spin series, we should lose nine consecutive spins on a random wheel 1 time.

322 x 9 = 2,898 spins

Out of 2,898 spins, we should have one "Streak of 9" (not accounting for dealer consistency, unbalanced wheel, etc.).

On a Streak of 9 with a $5 starting bet, a team will lose $1,875 on those nine spins:

Player 1 – wins $5 on all nine bets as he continues to win: $5 x 9 = $45

Player 2 – loses $5 + $10 + $15 + $30 + $60 + $120 + $240 + $480 + $960 = $1,920

$45 profits - $1,920 losses = $1,875 in losses

As this should occur over 9 spins out of 2,898, the team will lose $1,875 on those 9 spins.

On the remaining 2,889 spins, the team should average a profit on each spin. As you will see in the next chapter, a team should average anywhere from $3.00 to $3.50 per spin in most winning sessions. I have had sessions where the average per spin was around $2.90 and sessions where it was $3.80, but in general, it will be toward the middle of that range. Using the low end of that speculation, we can determine that the team should make a profit of $8,667 +/- over that same period:

2,889 spins x $3.00 per spin = $8,667 profit

$8,667 profit - $1,875 losses = $6,792 profit over 2,898 total spins

$6,792 profit / 2,898 total spins = $2.34 per spin lifetime average (remember, this is based on the low end of the average so it could actually be much higher)

Simply betting $5 to start on each session and following the Keefer Roulette System, each team should be able to average at least $2.34 per spin for each and every spin they play. There is no other game where you can be certain of how much you should make per hand at a table game or per spin on a slot machine. This system is so accurate that, without watching any part of a session, a team could tell me what stakes they played and how many spins they played and I would be able to give an accurate estimate of how much profit they made over those spins. In the next chapter, we will explore some actual results of my live trials and on the corresponding bar graphs, you will be able to visualize exactly how consistently my system builds profits over time! But before we do, let's look at the same mathematic principles applied to the Martingale System:

100% of results / .59% chance of losing eight consecutive spins (remember, with the Martingale System, you will reach the table max after eight losses) = 169.49

This means that out of 169 eight-spin series, we should lose eight consecutive spins on a random wheel 1 time.

$$169 \times 8 = 1,352 \text{ spins}$$

Out of 1,352 spins, we should have 1 Streak of 8 (not accounting for dealer consistency, unbalanced wheel, etc.). I hope you can already see an advantage of using the Keefer Roulette System over the Martingale System—with the Keefer System, you only lose once out of every 2,898 spins and with the Martingale System you lose more frequently, once out of every 1,352 spins!

On a Streak of 8 with a $5 starting bet, a Martingale player will lose $1,275.

Player 1 – loses $5 + $10 + $20 + $40 + $80 + $160 + $320 + $640 = $1,275

As this should occur over 8 spins out of 1,352, the player will lose $1,275 on those 8 spins.

On the remaining 1,344 spins, the player should hit his number roughly 47.37% of the time, earning $5 each time, and will break even on the remaining 52.63% of spins (as long as he finally hits a winning number).

1,344 spins x 47.37% = 637 winning spins
637 winning spins x $5 = $3,185
1,344 spins x 52.63% = 707 losing spins
707 losing spins x $0 = $0
$3,185 profit - $1,275 losses = $1,910 profit over 1,352 spins
$1,910 profit / 1,352 total spins = $1.41 per spin lifetime average

As for the Martingale System, it can still be profitable, but you will definitely earn at least 65% more profits with the Keefer Roulette System.

CHAPTER 4

EXAMPLES AND ACTUAL RESULTS

After coming up with the Keefer Roulette System, I immediately wanted to put it to use and see how effective—and profitable—it could be. My first seven sessions were played at a casino using an electronic roulette table. This table had a spinning wheel that automatically spun the ball each time, and therefore, there was no dealer. All bets were placed on a digital screen so the betting, payouts, and spins were all done fairly quickly.

Over my first seven sessions, I was able to net $1,870 in profits over a span of 13 hours and 15 minutes (an average of $141.13 per hour)! Over these 13 hours, 583 spins were performed, and I was able to average $3.21 per spin. Depending on the dealer, the other players, et cetera, each table will average a varying number of spins per hour. For this reason, I think it is important to display most data from my sessions as "average earnings per spin." On winning sessions, I tend to average anywhere from $3.00/spin to $3.50/spin. Therefore, if a dealer averages 25 spins per hour, you should expect earnings of $75-$88 per hour. However, if he is faster and averages 40 spins per hour, you can then expect to earn between $120 and $140 per hour! This makes table selection extremely important as it can really affect your profits!

During each session that I play, I record each spin in a ledger. In the first seven sessions, only "Even" or "Odd" was recorded. Since then, I began to also keep track of the actual number that was spun, not just whether it was Even or Odd. Examples 1-7 display the results of my initial sessions played over a period of a few days. Each chart portrays the bet amount of each player, the result of the spin, the profit or loss on that particular spin, and the balance of how much I was up during the session to that point. These charts show exactly how following the Keefer Roulette System gradually and consistently builds revenue over time. You will also find a bar graph after each chart, showing the accumulated profit of the session as it progressed. These graphs will give a visual perspective of how my profits were rising at a steady pace and will serve as an example of how your profits will grow as well! The trend line drawn on each graph distinctly portrays the direct correlation between number of spins and total profit. In other words, the more spins you play using my system, the more money you will make!

Example 1

Spins played: 87

Time played: 2 hours

Total profit: $230

Average $ per hour: $115.00

Average $ per spin: $2.64

Example 1: The Keefer Roulette System					
Spin	Player 1's Bet (Even)	Player 2's Bet (Odd)	Outcome	Profit/Loss	Balance
1	-	$5	Odd	$5	$5
2	-	$5	Odd	$5	$10
3	-	$5	Odd	$5	$15
4	-	$5	Even	($5)	$10
5	$5	$10	Odd	$5	$15
6	$10	$5	Even	$5	$20
7	$5	$10	Odd	$5	$25
8	$10	$5	Odd	($5)	$20
9	$15	$5	Odd	($10)	$10
10	$30	$5	Odd	($25)	($15)
11	$60	$5	Odd	($55)	($70)
12	$120	$5	Odd	($115)	($185)
13	$240	$5	Even	$235	$50
14	$5	$10	Odd	$5	$55
15	$10	$5	Even	$5	$60
16	$5	$10	Even	($5)	$55
17	$5	$15	Even	($10)	$45
18	$5	$30	Even	($25)	$20
19	$5	$60	Even	($55)	($35)
20	$5	$120	Odd	$115	$80
21	$10	$5	Even	$5	$85
22	$5	$10	Odd	$5	$90
23	$10	$5	Odd	($5)	$85

24	$15	$5	Even	$10	$95
25	$5	$10	Even	($5)	$90
26	$5	$15	Odd	$10	$100
27	$10	$5	Zero	($15)	$85
28	$15	$10	Even	$5	$90
29	$5	$15	Even	($10)	$80
30	$5	$30	Odd	$25	$105
31	$10	$5	Even	$5	$110
32	$5	$10	Odd	$5	$115
33	$10	$5	Even	$5	$120
34	$5	$10	Odd	$5	$125
35	$10	$5	Even	$5	$130
36	$5	$10	Odd	$5	$135
37	$10	$5	Odd	($5)	$130
38	$15	$5	Even	$10	$140
39	$5	$10	Odd	$5	$145
40	$10	$5	Even	$5	$150
41	$5	$10	Odd	$5	$155
42	$10	$5	Even	$5	$160
43	$5	$10	Odd	$5	$165
44	$10	$5	Odd	($5)	$160
45	$15	$5	Even	$10	$170
46	$5	$10	Odd	$5	$175
47	$10	$5	Odd	($5)	$170
48	$15	$5	Even	$10	$180
49	$5	$10	Odd	$5	$185
50	$10	$5	Even	$5	$190
51	$5	$10	Even	($5)	$185
52	$5	$15	Even	($10)	$175
53	$5	$30	Odd	$25	$200
54	$10	$5	Even	$5	$205
55	$5	$10	Even	($5)	$200
56	$5	$15	Odd	$10	$210
57	$10	$5	Zero	($15)	$195
58	$15	$10	Even	$5	$200

59	$5	$15	Even	($10)	$190
60	$5	$30	Odd	($25)	$165
61	$10	$5	Odd	($5)	$160
62	$15	$5	Odd	($10)	$150
63	$30	$5	Odd	($25)	$125
64	$60	$5	Odd	($55)	$70
65	$120	$5	Odd	($115)	($45)
66	$240	$5	Even	$235	$190
67	$5	$10	Even	($5)	$185
68	$5	$15	Zero	($20)	$165
69	$10	$30	Odd	$20	$185
70	$15	$5	Odd	($10)	$175
71	$30	$5	Even	$25	$200
72	$5	$10	Even	($5)	$195
73	$5	$15	Odd	$10	$205
74	$10	$5	Odd	($5)	$200
75	$15	$5	Even	$10	$210
76	$5	$10	Odd	$5	$215
77	$10	$5	Even	$5	$220
78	$5	$10	Even	($5)	$215
79	$5	$15	Odd	$10	$225
80	$10	$5	Odd	($5)	$220
81	$15	$5	Zero	($20)	$200
82	$30	$10	Zero	($40)	$160
83	$60	$15	Even	$45	$205
84	$5	$30	Odd	$25	$230
85	$10	$5	Zero	($15)	$215
86	$15	$10	Even	$5	$220
87	$5	$15	Odd	$10	$230

PROFIT DURING SESSION (SPINS 1-87)

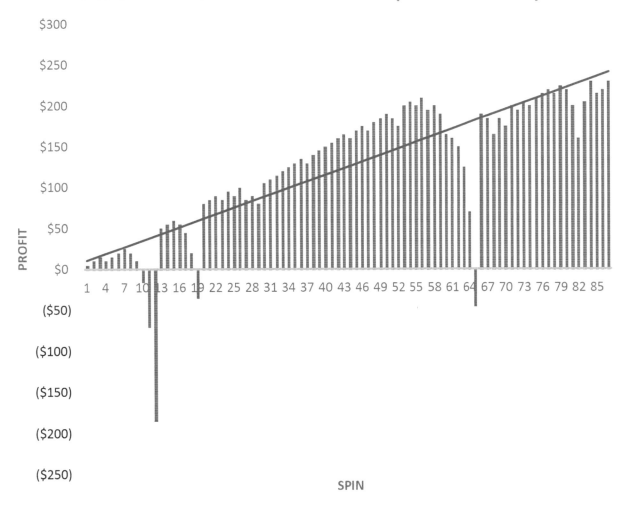

Notes: Take note of the gradual increase in profit over time (spins played). On every one of these graphs you will see some brief areas where the graph dips. This portrays what happens when a streak occurs. Streaks are not desirable as it means one of the players is losing increasingly larger, consecutive bets while the other player is winning a small amount each spin. As long streaks are the only way you will lose money with my system, the graph shows how you also get right back on track as soon as the streak ends.

Example 2

Spins played: 132

Time played: 3 hours

Total profit: $490

Average $ per hour: $163.33

Average $ per spin: $3.71

Example 2: The Keefer Roulette System					
Spin	Player 1's Bet (Even)	Player 2's Bet (Odd)	Outcome	Profit/Loss	Balance
1	-	$5	Even	($5)	($5)
2	$5	$10	Odd	$5	$0
3	$10	$5	Odd	($5)	($5)
4	$15	$5	Even	$10	$5
5	$5	$10	Odd	$5	$10
6	$10	$5	Even	$5	$15
7	$5	$10	Even	($5)	$10
8	$5	$15	Even	($10)	$0
9	$5	$30	Odd	$25	$25
10	$10	$5	Odd	($5)	$20
11	$15	$5	Even	$10	$30
12	$5	$10	Even	($5)	$25
13	$5	$15	Odd	$10	$35
14	$10	$5	Even	$5	$40
15	$5	$10	Even	($5)	$35
16	$5	$15	Even	($10)	$25
17	$5	$30	Even	($25)	$0
18	$5	$60	Even	($55)	($55)
19	$5	$120	Odd	$115	$60
20	$10	$5	Even	$5	$65
21	$5	$10	Odd	$5	$70
22	$10	$5	Even	$5	$75

23	$5	$10	Zero	$15	$90
24	$10	$15	Odd	$5	$95
25	$15	$5	Odd	($10)	$85
26	$30	$5	Even	$25	$110
27	$5	$10	Zero	($15)	$95
28	$10	$15	Odd	$5	$100
29	$15	$5	Even	$10	$110
30	$5	$10	Odd	$5	$115
31	$10	$5	Odd	($5)	$110
32	$15	$5	Odd	($10)	$100
33	$30	$5	Even	$25	$125
34	$5	$10	Even	($5)	$120
35	$5	$15	Even	($10)	$110
36	$5	$30	Odd	$25	$135
37	$10	$5	Odd	($5)	$130
38	$15	$5	Odd	($10)	$120
39	$30	$5	Even	$25	$145
40	$5	$10	Odd	$5	$150
41	$10	$5	Even	$5	$155
42	$5	$10	Odd	$5	$160
43	$10	$5	Odd	($5)	$155
44	$15	$5	Even	$10	$165
45	$5	$10	Even	($5)	$160
46	$5	$15	Even	($10)	$150
47	$5	$30	Odd	$25	$175
48	$10	$5	Even	$5	$180
49	$5	$10	Even	($5)	$175
50	$5	$15	Even	($10)	$165
51	$5	$30	Even	($25)	$140
52	$5	$60	Even	($55)	$85
53	$5	$120	Even	($115)	($30)
54	$5	$240	Odd	$235	$205
55	$10	$5	Odd	($5)	$200
56	$15	$5	Even	$10	$210
57	$5	$10	Odd	$5	$215

58	$10	$5	Zero	($15)	$200
59	$15	$10	Odd	($5)	$195
60	$30	$5	Even	$25	$220
61	$5	$10	Odd	$5	$225
62	$10	$5	Even	$5	$230
63	$5	$10	Even	($5)	$225
64	$5	$15	Even	($10)	$215
65	$5	$30	Odd	$25	$240
66	$10	$5	Even	$5	$245
67	$5	$10	Odd	$5	$250
68	$10	$5	Odd	($5)	$245
69	$15	$5	Zero	($20)	$225
70	$30	$10	Even	$20	$245
71	$5	$15	Odd	$10	$255
72	$10	$5	Even	$5	$260
73	$5	$10	Odd	$5	$265
74	$10	$5	Even	$5	$270
75	$5	$10	Odd	$5	$275
76	$10	$5	Even	$5	$280
77	$5	$10	Even	($5)	$275
78	$5	$15	Even	($10)	$265
79	$5	$30	Even	($25)	$240
80	$5	$60	Even	($55)	$185
81	$5	$120	Odd	$115	$300
82	$10	$5	Even	$5	$305
83	$5	$10	Even	($5)	$300
84	$5	$15	Even	($10)	$290
85	$5	$30	Even	($25)	$265
86	$5	$60	Even	($55)	$210
87	$5	$120	Even	($115)	$95
88	$5	$240	Zero	($245)	($150)
89	$10	$480	Even	($470)	($620)
90	$5	$960	Odd	$955	$335
91	$10	$5	Odd	($5)	$330
92	$15	$5	Zero	($20)	$310

93	$30	$10	Odd	($20)	$290
94	$60	$5	Odd	($55)	$235
95	$120	$5	Even	$115	$350
96	$5	$10	Odd	$5	$355
97	$10	$5	Odd	($5)	$350
98	$15	$5	Even	$10	$360
99	$5	$10	Odd	$5	$365
100	$10	$5	Odd	($5)	$360
101	$15	$5	Even	$10	$370
102	$5	$10	Odd	$5	$375
103	$10	$5	Even	$5	$380
104	$5	$10	Odd	$5	$385
105	$10	$5	Even	$5	$390
106	$5	$10	Odd	$5	$395
107	$10	$5	Odd	($5)	$390
108	$15	$5	Odd	($10)	$380
109	$30	$5	Even	$25	$405
110	$5	$10	Odd	$5	$410
111	$10	$5	Odd	($5)	$405
112	$15	$5	Odd	($10)	$395
113	$30	$5	Zero	($35)	$360
114	$60	$10	Odd	($50)	$310
115	$120	$5	Odd	($115)	$195
116	$240	$5	Odd	($235)	($40)
117	$480	$5	Odd	($475)	($515)
118	$960	$5	Even	$955	$440
119	$5	$10	Even	($5)	$435
120	$5	$15	Even	($10)	$425
121	$5	$30	Even	($25)	$400
122	$5	$60	Odd	$55	$455
123	$10	$5	Odd	($5)	$450
124	$15	$5	Even	$10	$460
125	$5	$10	Even	($5)	$455
126	$5	$15	Even	($10)	$445
127	$5	$30	Odd	$25	$470

128	$10	$5	Odd	($5)	$465
129	$15	$5	Odd	($10)	$455
130	$30	$5	Odd	($25)	$430
131	$60	$5	Odd	($55)	$375
132	$120	$5	Even	$115	$490

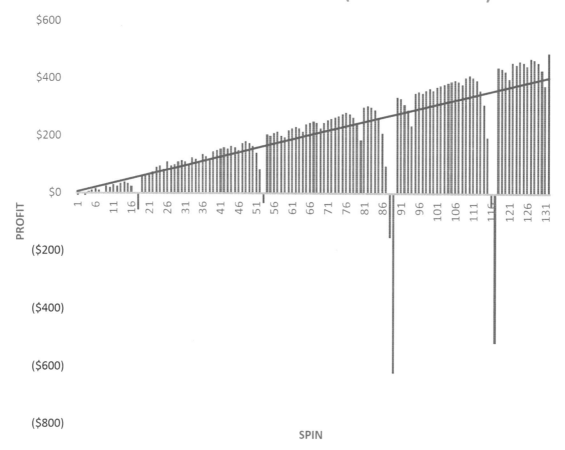

PROFIT DURING SESSION (SPINS 1-132)

Notes: This was a longer session at three hours. In this time, we had two bad streaks where we almost lost a bet nine consecutive times. You can see these two streaks on the graph above where the profit is very nice, but plummets into the negative. When this occurred, we actually had less money than we initially brought to the table, but since the system was adhered to, an Odd number did hit just in time and all losses from previous spins were recovered. It can be a stressful situation realizing that your bets continue to increase only to get your lost bets back, but following the system gives you the best chance for consistent profits. Also remember that there will be times—few as they may be—where you will have a losing session. However, these losing sessions will be at a minimum and as long as you are experiencing at least five winning sessions for each losing session, you will make money in the long-run. As was said before, it is crucial to already know in your mind that you will occasionally lose money with this system as it is based on a high probability, not a certainty.

Example 3

Spins played: 45

Time played: 1 hour

Total profit: $135.00

Average $ per hour: $135.00

Average $ per spin: $3.00

\multicolumn{6}{c}{**Example 3: The Keefer Roulette System**}					
Spin	Player 1's Bet (Even)	Player 2's Bet (Odd)	Outcome	Profit/Loss	Balance
1	$5	-	Even	$5	$5
2	$5	-	Even	$5	$10
3	$5	-	Odd	($5)	$5
4	$10	$5	Odd	($5)	$0
5	$15	$5	Even	$10	$10
6	$5	$10	Even	($5)	$5
7	$5	$15	Even	($10)	($5)
8	$5	$30	Even	($25)	($30)
9	$5	$60	Odd	$55	$25
10	$10	$5	Odd	($5)	$20
11	$15	$5	Even	$10	$30
12	$5	$10	Even	($5)	$25
13	$5	$15	Even	($10)	$15
14	$5	$30	Even	($25)	($10)
15	$5	$60	Odd	$55	$45
16	$10	$5	Odd	($5)	$40
17	$15	$5	Zero	($20)	$20
18	$30	$10	Even	$20	$40
19	$5	$15	Odd	$10	$50
20	$10	$5	Odd	($5)	$45
21	$15	$5	Odd	($10)	$35
22	$30	$5	Odd	($25)	$10
23	$60	$5	Even	$55	$65

24	$5	$10	Even	($5)	$60
25	$5	$15	Even	($10)	$50
26	$5	$30	Even	($25)	$25
27	$5	$60	Odd	$55	$80
28	$10	$5	Zero	($15)	$65
29	$15	$10	Even	$5	$70
30	$5	$15	Even	($10)	$60
31	$5	$30	Even	($25)	$35
32	$5	$60	Zero	($65)	($30)
33	$10	$120	Odd	$110	$80
34	$15	$5	Odd	($10)	$70
35	$30	$5	Odd	($25)	$45
36	$60	$5	Zero	($65)	($20)
37	$120	$10	Odd	($110)	($130)
38	$240	$5	Odd	($235)	($365)
39	$480	$5	Even	$475	$110
40	$5	$10	Even	($5)	$105
41	$5	$15	Even	($10)	$95
42	$5	$30	Even	($25)	$70
43	$5	$60	Even	($55)	$15
44	$5	$120	Even	($115)	($100)
45	$5	$240	Odd	$235	$135

PROFIT DURING SESSION (SPINS 1-45)

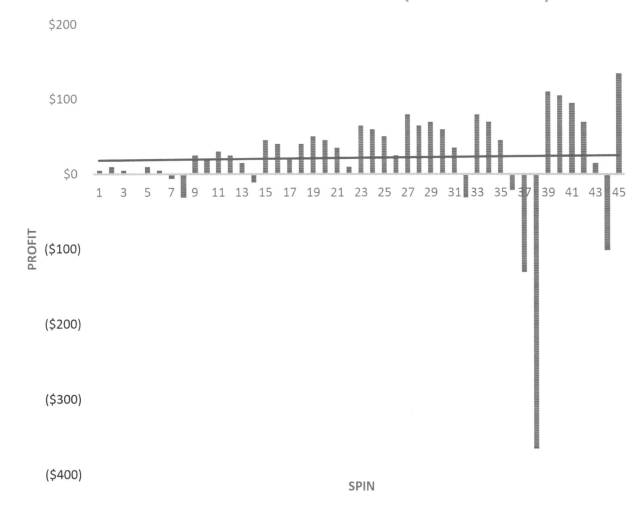

Notes: This trend line is not as positive as the first two examples. In this shorter session, there were many streaks where we lost 4, 5, or 6 straight spins. Frequent streaks like these will skew your results somewhat, but as you can see, it was still a very profitable session. When a table tends to be streaky as this one was, it is usually a good idea to limit your spins or playing time as you may run into longer, more devastating streaks that could result in a losing session. Remember, the best tables you can play at are the ones that produce completely random results!

Example 4

Spins played: 138

Time played: 3 hours 10 minutes

Total profit: $425.00

Average $ per hour: $134.07

Average $ per spin: $3.08

Spin	Player 1's Bet (Even)	Player 2's Bet (Odd)	Outcome	Profit/Loss	Balance
- Example 4: The Keefer Roulette System
1	$5	-	Even	$5	$5
2	$5	-	Odd	($5)	$0
3	$10	$5	Even	$5	$5
4	$5	$10	Even	($5)	$0
5	$5	$15	Even	($10)	($10)
6	$5	$30	Zero	($35)	($45)
7	$10	$60	Odd	$50	$5
8	$15	$5	Odd	($10)	($5)
9	$30	$5	Odd	($25)	($30)
10	$60	$5	Zero	($65)	($95)
11	$120	$10	Even	$110	$15
12	$5	$15	Zero	($20)	($5)
13	$10	$30	Even	($20)	($25)
14	$5	$60	Even	($55)	($80)
15	$5	$120	Even	($115)	($195)
16	$5	$240	Zero	($245)	($440)
17	$10	$480	Odd	$470	$30
18	$15	$5	Odd	($10)	$20
19	$30	$5	Odd	($25)	($5)
20	$60	$5	Even	$55	$50
21	$5	$10	Even	($5)	$45
22	$5	$15	Odd	$10	$55
23	$10	$5	Odd	($5)	$50

24	$15	$5	Even	$10	$60
25	$5	$10	Even	($5)	$55
26	$5	$15	Odd	$10	$65
27	$10	$5	Even	$5	$70
28	$5	$10	Even	($5)	$65
29	$5	$15	Odd	$10	$75
30	$10	$5	Zero	($15)	$60
31	$15	$10	Even	$5	$65
32	$5	$15	Odd	$10	$75
33	$10	$5	Even	$5	$80
34	$5	$10	Odd	$5	$85
35	$10	$5	Even	$5	$90
36	$5	$10	Even	($5)	$85
37	$5	$15	Odd	$10	$95
38	$10	$5	Odd	($5)	$90
39	$15	$5	Odd	($10)	$80
40	$30	$5	Odd	($25)	$55
41	$60	$5	Even	$55	$110
42	$5	$10	Odd	$5	$115
43	$10	$5	Even	$5	$120
44	$5	$10	Even	($5)	$115
45	$5	$15	Zero	($20)	$95
46	$10	$30	Even	($20)	$75
47	$5	$60	Zero	($65)	$10
48	$10	$120	Odd	$110	$120
49	$15	$5	Odd	($10)	$110
50	$30	$5	Odd	($25)	$85
51	$60	$5	Even	$55	$140
52	$5	$10	Even	($5)	$135
53	$5	$15	Odd	$10	$145
54	$10	$5	Odd	($5)	$140
55	$15	$5	Even	$10	$150
56	$5	$10	Even	($5)	$145
57	$5	$15	Even	($10)	$135
58	$5	$30	Even	($25)	$110

59	$5	$60	Even	($55)	$55
60	$5	$120	Odd	$115	$170
61	$10	$5	Odd	($5)	$165
62	$15	$5	Odd	($10)	$155
63	$30	$5	Even	$25	$180
64	$5	$10	Odd	$5	$185
65	$10	$5	Even	$5	$190
66	$5	$10	Even	($5)	$185
67	$5	$15	Even	($10)	$175
68	$5	$30	Odd	$25	$200
69	$10	$5	Zero	($15)	$185
70	$15	$10	Even	$5	$190
71	$5	$15	Odd	$10	$200
72	$10	$5	Even	$5	$205
73	$5	$10	Even	($5)	$200
74	$5	$15	Zero	($20)	$180
75	$10	$30	Even	($20)	$160
76	$5	$60	Even	($55)	$105
77	$5	$120	Odd	$115	$220
78	$10	$5	Odd	($5)	$215
79	$15	$5	Even	$10	$225
80	$5	$10	Odd	$5	$230
81	$10	$5	Odd	($5)	$225
82	$15	$5	Odd	($10)	$215
83	$30	$5	Even	$25	$240
84	$5	$10	Odd	$5	$245
85	$10	$5	Odd	($5)	$240
86	$15	$5	Even	$10	$250
87	$5	$10	Odd	$5	$255
88	$10	$5	Odd	($5)	$250
89	$15	$5	Odd	($10)	$240
90	$30	$5	Odd	($25)	$215
91	$60	$5	Even	$55	$270
92	$5	$10	Even	($5)	$265
93	$5	$15	Even	($10)	$255

94	$5	$30	Even	($25)	$230
95	$5	$60	Odd	$55	$285
96	$10	$5	Even	$5	$290
97	$5	$10	Odd	$5	$295
98	$10	$5	Odd	($5)	$290
99	$15	$5	Odd	($10)	$280
100	$30	$5	Even	$25	$305
101	$5	$10	Odd	$5	$310
102	$10	$5	Odd	($5)	$305
103	$15	$5	Odd	($10)	$295
104	$30	$5	Zero	($35)	$260
105	$60	$10	Even	$50	$310
106	$5	$15	Even	($10)	$300
107	$5	$30	Even	($25)	$275
108	$5	$60	Even	($55)	$220
109	$5	$120	Odd	$115	$335
110	$10	$5	Odd	($5)	$330
111	$15	$5	Odd	($10)	$320
112	$30	$5	Even	$25	$345
113	$5	$10	Even	($5)	$340
114	$5	$15	Even	($10)	$330
115	$5	$30	Even	($25)	$305
116	$5	$60	Odd	$55	$360
117	$10	$5	Odd	($5)	$355
118	$15	$5	Even	$10	$365
119	$5	$10	Even	($5)	$360
120	$5	$15	Even	($10)	$350
121	$5	$30	Odd	$25	$375
122	$10	$5	Even	$5	$380
123	$5	$10	Even	($5)	$375
124	$5	$15	Odd	$10	$385
125	$10	$5	Odd	($5)	$380
126	$15	$5	Odd	($10)	$370
127	$30	$5	Odd	($25)	$345
128	$60	$5	Even	$55	$400

129	$5	$10	Even	($5)	$395
130	$5	$15	Even	($10)	$385
131	$5	$30	Even	($25)	$360
132	$5	$60	Even	($55)	$305
133	$5	$120	Even	($115)	$190
134	$5	$240	Odd	$235	$425
135	$10	$5	Zero	($15)	$410
136	$15	$10	Odd	($5)	$405
137	$30	$5	Even	$25	$430
138	$5	$10	Even	($5)	$425

PROFIT DURING SESSION (SPINS 1-138)

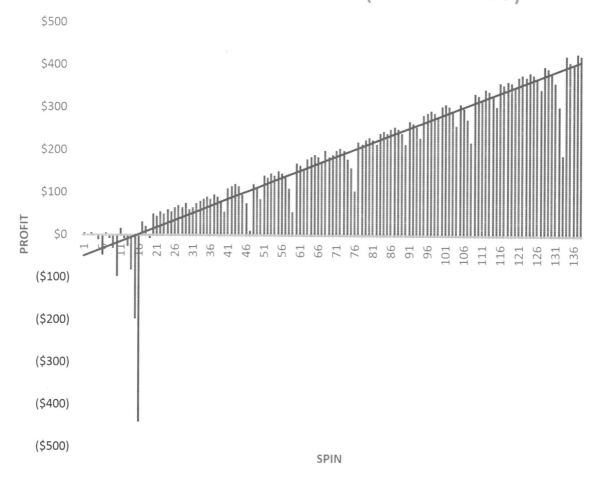

Notes: This session got off to a bad start. There were 4 Zeroes (0 or 00) in the first 16 spins. In fact, there were 11 Zeroes in all during this 138-spin session. Theoretical probability says there should be 7 Zeroes or double-Zeroes spun over the course of 138 spins. Naturally, this number will be high in some sessions and low in others, but even with a high Zero-count, we still averaged over $3.00 per spin.

Example 5

Spins played: 33

Time played: 50 minutes

Total profit: $100.00

Average $ per hour: $120.00

Average $ per spin: $3.03

\multicolumn{6}{c}{**Example 5: The Keefer Roulette System**}
Spin	Player 1's Bet (Even)	Player 2's Bet (Odd)	Outcome	Profit/Loss	Balance
1	$5	-	Odd	($5)	($5)
2	$10	$5	Even	$5	$0
3	$5	$10	Even	($5)	($5)
4	$5	$15	Even	($10)	($15)
5	$5	$30	Even	($25)	($40)
6	$5	$60	Odd	$55	$15
7	$10	$5	Even	$5	$20
8	$5	$10	Even	($5)	$15
9	$5	$15	Zero	($20)	($5)
10	$10	$30	Odd	$20	$15
11	$15	$5	Odd	($10)	$5
12	$30	$5	Odd	($25)	($20)
13	$60	$5	Odd	($55)	($75)
14	$120	$5	Odd	($115)	($190)
15	$240	$5	Odd	($235)	($425)
16	$480	$5	Even	$475	$50
17	$5	$10	Zero	($15)	$35
18	$10	$15	Odd	$5	$40
19	$15	$5	Odd	($10)	$30
20	$30	$5	Odd	($25)	$5
21	$60	$5	Even	$55	$60
22	$5	$10	Even	($5)	$55
23	$5	$15	Odd	$10	$65

24	$10	$5	Odd	($5)	$60
25	$15	$5	Odd	($10)	$50
26	$30	$5	Even	$25	$75
27	$5	$10	Even	($5)	$70
28	$5	$15	Odd	$10	$80
29	$10	$5	Even	$5	$85
30	$5	$10	Odd	$5	$90
31	$10	$5	Odd	($5)	$85
32	$15	$5	Odd	($10)	$75
33	$30	$5	Even	$25	$100

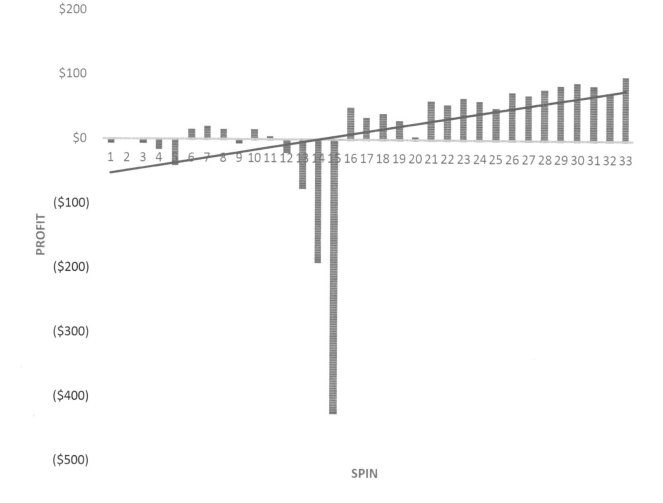

PROFIT DURING SESSION (SPINS 1-33)

Notes: This was one of the shortest sessions I have played. Even with a slow start and a 7-streak toward the middle, I was still able to average over $100 per hour and over $3.00 per spin.

Example 6

Spins played: 48

Time played: 1 hour

Total profit: $150.00

Average $ per hour: $150.00

Average $ per spin: $3.13

Example 6: The Keefer Roulette System					
Spin	Player 1's Bet (Even)	Player 2's Bet (Odd)	Outcome	Profit/Loss	Balance
1	$5	-	Even	$5	$5
2	$5	-	Zero	($5)	$0
3	$10	$5	Odd	($5)	($5)
4	$15	$5	Odd	($10)	($15)
5	$30	$5	Even	$25	$10
6	$5	$10	Odd	$5	$15
7	$10	$5	Even	$5	$20
8	$5	$10	Odd	$5	$25
9	$10	$5	Odd	($5)	$20
10	$15	$5	Odd	($10)	$10
11	$30	$5	Odd	($25)	($15)
12	$60	$5	Even	$55	$40
13	$5	$10	Even	($5)	$35
14	$5	$15	Odd	$10	$45
15	$10	$5	Even	$5	$50
16	$5	$10	Zero	($15)	$35
17	$10	$15	Odd	$5	$40
18	$15	$5	Even	$10	$50
19	$5	$10	Odd	$5	$55
20	$10	$5	Zero	($15)	$40
21	$15	$10	Odd	($5)	$35
22	$30	$5	Even	$25	$60
23	$5	$10	Even	($5)	$55

24	$5	$15	Odd	$10	$65
25	$10	$5	Zero	($15)	$50
26	$15	$10	Even	$5	$55
27	$5	$15	Even	($10)	$45
28	$5	$30	Odd	$25	$70
29	$10	$5	Odd	($5)	$65
30	$15	$5	Odd	($10)	$55
31	$30	$5	Odd	($25)	$30
32	$60	$5	Even	$55	$85
33	$5	$10	Odd	$5	$90
34	$10	$5	Even	$5	$95
35	$5	$10	Even	($5)	$90
36	$5	$15	Even	($10)	$80
37	$5	$30	Even	($25)	$55
38	$5	$60	Even	($55)	$0
39	$5	$120	Even	($115)	($115)
40	$5	$240	Even	($235)	($350)
41	$5	$480	Even	($475)	($825)
42	$5	$960	Odd	$955	$130
43	$10	$5	Odd	($5)	$125
44	$15	$5	Odd	($10)	$115
45	$30	$5	Even	$25	$140
46	$5	$10	Odd	$5	$145
47	$10	$5	Odd	($5)	$140
48	$15	$5	Even	$10	$150

PROFIT DURING SESSION (SPINS 1-48)

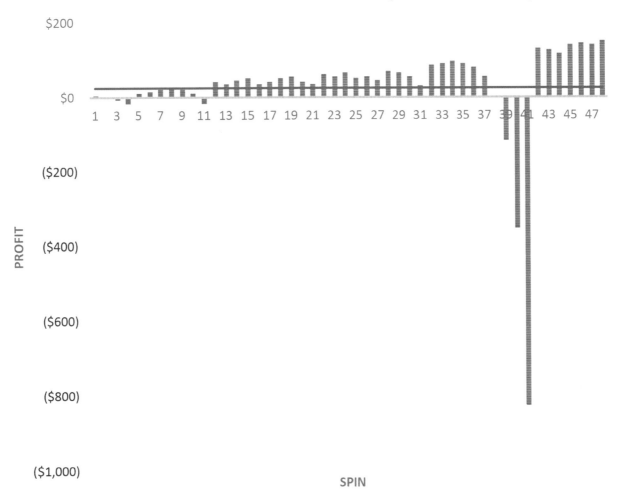

Notes: At one point, we lost eight spins in a row on one bet and almost lost for the session. Fortunately, we finally hit an Odd number on the ninth try and fully recovered. You will have times where this happens and it definitely gets your adrenaline rushing! Just stick to the plan and let the odds work themselves out!

Example 7

Spins played: 100

Time played: 2 hours 15 minutes

Total profit: $340.00

Average $ per hour: $151.11

Average $ per spin: $3.40

\multicolumn{6}{c}{**Example 7: The Keefer Roulette System**}
Spin	Player 1's Bet (Even)	Player 2's Bet (Odd)	Outcome	Profit/Loss	Balance
1	-	$5	Odd	$5	$5
2	-	$5	Odd	$5	$10
3	-	$5	Even	($5)	$5
4	$5	$10	Even	($5)	$0
5	$5	$15	Even	($10)	($10)
6	$5	$30	Odd	$25	$15
7	$10	$5	Even	$5	$20
8	$5	$10	Even	($5)	$15
9	$5	$15	Odd	$10	$25
10	$10	$5	Even	$5	$30
11	$5	$10	Odd	$5	$35
12	$10	$5	Even	$5	$40
13	$5	$10	Even	($5)	$35
14	$5	$15	Odd	$10	$45
15	$10	$5	Even	$5	$50
16	$5	$10	Even	($5)	$45
17	$5	$15	Even	($10)	$35
18	$5	$30	Zero	($35)	$0
19	$10	$60	Even	($50)	($50)
20	$5	$120	Odd	$115	$65
21	$10	$5	Even	$5	$70
22	$5	$10	Even	($5)	$65
23	$5	$15	Odd	$10	$75

24	$10	$5	Even	$5	$80
25	$5	$10	Even	($5)	$75
26	$5	$15	Even	($10)	$65
27	$5	$30	Even	($25)	$40
28	$5	$60	Odd	$55	$95
29	$10	$5	Even	$5	$100
30	$5	$10	Even	($5)	$95
31	$5	$15	Even	($10)	$85
32	$5	$30	Odd	$25	$110
33	$10	$5	Even	$5	$115
34	$5	$10	Even	($5)	$110
35	$5	$15	Odd	$10	$120
36	$10	$5	Even	$5	$125
37	$5	$10	Even	($5)	$120
38	$5	$15	Odd	$10	$130
39	$10	$5	Odd	($5)	$125
40	$15	$5	Odd	($10)	$115
41	$30	$5	Even	$25	$140
42	$5	$10	Odd	$5	$145
43	$10	$5	Even	$5	$150
44	$5	$10	Even	($5)	$145
45	$5	$15	Even	($10)	$135
46	$5	$30	Odd	$25	$160
47	$10	$5	Odd	($5)	$155
48	$15	$5	Even	$10	$165
49	$5	$10	Zero	($15)	$150
50	$10	$15	Even	($5)	$145
51	$5	$30	Odd	$25	$170
52	$10	$5	Odd	($5)	$165
53	$15	$5	Even	$10	$175
54	$5	$10	Even	($5)	$170
55	$5	$15	Even	($10)	$160
56	$5	$30	Even	($25)	$135
57	$5	$60	Odd	$55	$190
58	$10	$5	Even	$5	$195

59	$5	$10	Odd	$5	$200
60	$10	$5	Odd	($5)	$195
61	$15	$5	Even	$10	$205
62	$5	$10	Odd	$5	$210
63	$10	$5	Zero	($15)	$195
64	$15	$10	Odd	($5)	$190
65	$30	$5	Odd	($25)	$165
66	$60	$5	Even	$55	$220
67	$5	$10	Even	($5)	$215
68	$5	$15	Even	($10)	$205
69	$5	$30	Zero	($35)	$170
70	$10	$60	Odd	$50	$220
71	$15	$5	Even	$10	$230
72	$5	$10	Even	($5)	$225
73	$5	$15	Odd	$10	$235
74	$10	$5	Odd	($5)	$230
75	$15	$5	Zero	($20)	$210
76	$30	$10	Odd	($20)	$190
77	$60	$5	Odd	($55)	$135
78	$120	$5	Even	$115	$250
79	$5	$10	Odd	$5	$255
80	$10	$5	Even	$5	$260
81	$5	$10	Even	($5)	$255
82	$5	$15	Even	($10)	$245
83	$5	$30	Even	($25)	$220
84	$5	$60	Odd	$55	$275
85	$10	$5	Even	$5	$280
86	$5	$10	Even	($5)	$275
87	$5	$15	Odd	$10	$285
88	$10	$5	Odd	($5)	$280
89	$15	$5	Odd	($10)	$270
90	$30	$5	Odd	($25)	$245
91	$60	$5	Even	$55	$300
92	$5	$10	Odd	$5	$305
93	$10	$5	Even	$5	$310

94	$5	$10	Odd	$5	$315
95	$10	$5	Odd	($5)	$310
96	$15	$5	Even	$10	$320
97	$5	$10	Odd	$5	$325
98	$10	$5	Even	$5	$330
99	$5	$10	Odd	$5	$335
100	$10	$5	Even	$5	$340

PROFIT DURING SESSION (SPINS 1-100)

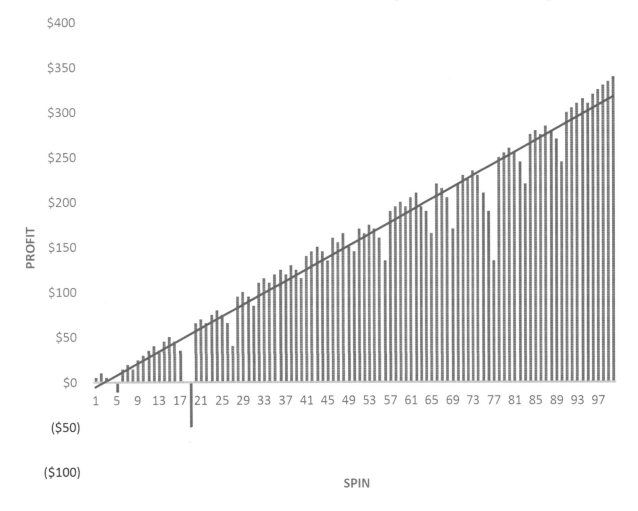

The next example was a long session (200 spins). Once again, the statistics were virtually identical, proving the accuracy and consistency of the Keefer Roulette System.

Example 8

Spins played: 200

Time played: 4 hours 15 minutes

Total profit: $610.00

Average $ per hour: $143.53

Average $ per spin: $3.05

Spin	Player 1's Bet (Black)	Player 2's Bet (Red)	Outcome	Profit/Loss	Balance
\multicolumn{6}{c}{Example 8: The Keefer Roulette System}					
1	$5	-	21	($5)	($5)
2	$10	$5	9	($5)	($10)
3	$15	$5	17	$10	$0
4	$5	$10	13	($5)	($5)
5	$5	$15	17	($10)	($15)
6	$5	$30	14	$25	$10
7	$10	$5	33	$5	$15
8	$5	$10	2	($5)	$10
9	$5	$15	16	$10	$20
10	$10	$5	34	($5)	$15
11	$15	$5	29	$10	$25
12	$5	$10	17	($5)	$20
13	$5	$15	16	$10	$30
14	$10	$5	9	($5)	$25
15	$15	$5	20	$10	$35
16	$5	$10	21	$5	$40
17	$10	$5	18	($5)	$35
18	$15	$5	21	($10)	$25
19	$30	$5	13	$25	$50
20	$5	$10	15	($5)	$45
21	$5	$15	4	($10)	$35
22	$5	$30	30	$25	$60
23	$10	$5	2	$5	$65

24	$5	$10	10	($5)	$60
25	$5	$15	14	$10	$70
26	$10	$5	22	$5	$75
27	$5	$10	23	$5	$80
28	$10	$5	15	$5	$85
29	$5	$10	27	$5	$90
30	$10	$5	30	($5)	$85
31	$15	$5	0	($20)	$65
32	$30	$10	0 0	($40)	$25
33	$60	$15	15	$45	$70
34	$5	$30	22	($25)	$45
35	$5	$60	2	($55)	($10)
36	$5	$120	7	$105	$95
37	$10	$5	21	($5)	$90
38	$15	$5	0 0	($20)	$70
39	$30	$10	13	$20	$90
40	$5	$15	2	($10)	$80
41	$5	$30	20	($25)	$55
42	$5	$60	20	($55)	$0
43	$5	$120	17	($115)	($115)
44	$5	$240	1	$235	$120
45	$10	$5	3	($5)	$115
46	$15	$5	21	($10)	$105
47	$30	$5	11	$25	$130
48	$5	$10	29	($5)	$125
49	$5	$15	23	$10	$135
50	$10	$5	5	($5)	$130

PROFIT DURING SESSION (SPINS 1-50)

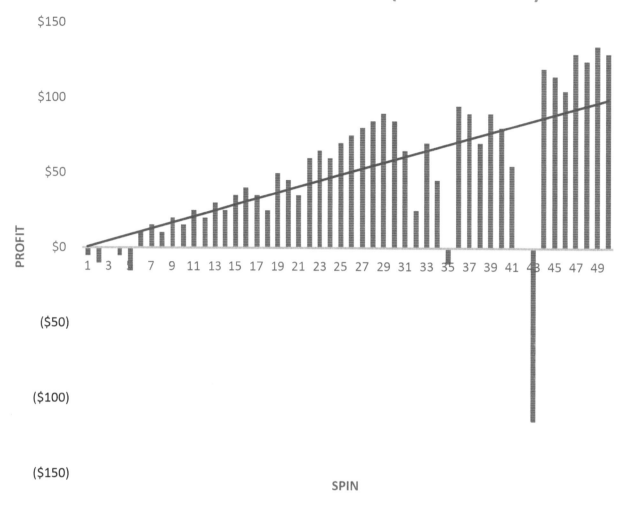

Spin	Player 1's Bet (Black)	Player 2's Bet (Red)	Outcome	Profit/Loss	Balance
			Example 8: The Keefer Roulette System (Continued)		
51	$15.00	$5.00	24	$10	$140
52	$5.00	$10.00	35	($5)	$135
53	$5.00	$15.00	35	($10)	$125
54	$5.00	$30.00	19	$25	$150
55	$10.00	$5.00	0	($15)	$135
56	$15.00	$10.00	8	$5	$140
57	$5.00	$15.00	29	($10)	$130
58	$5.00	$30.00	11	($25)	$105
59	$5.00	$60.00	21	$55	$160
60	$10.00	$5.00	2	$5	$165
61	$5.00	$10.00	27	$5	$170
62	$10.00	$5.00	31	$5	$175
63	$5.00	$10.00	4	($5)	$170
64	$5.00	$15.00	23	$10	$180
65	$10.00	$5.00	22	$5	$185
66	$5.00	$10.00	22	($5)	$180
67	$5.00	$15.00	13	($10)	$170
68	$5.00	$30.00	22	($25)	$145
69	$5.00	$60.00	16	$55	$200
70	$10.00	$5.00	19	($5)	$195
71	$15.00	$5.00	10	$10	$205
72	$5.00	$10.00	13	($5)	$200
73	$5.00	$15.00	15	($10)	$190
74	$5.00	$30.00	23	$25	$215
75	$10.00	$5.00	17	$5	$220
76	$5.00	$10.00	3	$5	$225
77	$10.00	$5.00	14	($5)	$220
78	$15.00	$5.00	7	($10)	$210
79	$30.00	$5.00	14	($25)	$185
80	$60.00	$5.00	31	$55	$240
81	$5.00	$10.00	8	($5)	$235

82	$5.00	$15.00	2	($10)	$225
83	$5.00	$30.00	5	$25	$250
84	$10.00	$5.00	26	$5	$255
85	$5.00	$10.00	16	$5	$260
86	$10.00	$5.00	28	$5	$265
87	$5.00	$10.00	22	($5)	$260
88	$5.00	$15.00	10	($10)	$250
89	$5.00	$30.00	33	($25)	$225
90	$5.00	$60.00	30	$55	$280
91	$10.00	$5.00	20	$5	$285
92	$5.00	$10.00	34	$5	$290
93	$10.00	$5.00	33	$5	$295
94	$5.00	$10.00	3	$5	$300
95	$10.00	$5.00	20	$5	$305
96	$5.00	$10.00	0	($15)	$290
97	$10.00	$15.00	3	$5	$295
98	$15.00	$5.00	28	$10	$305
99	$5.00	$10.00	2	($5)	$300
100	$5.00	$15.00	0	($20)	$280

PROFIT DURING SESSION (SPINS 1-100)

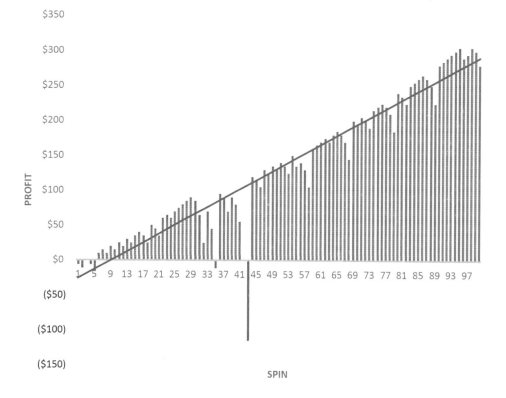

	Example 8: The Keefer Roulette System (Continued)				
Spin	Player 1's Bet (Black)	Player 2's Bet (Red)	Outcome	Profit/Loss	Balance
101	$10.00	$30.00	33	($20)	$260
102	$5.00	$60.00	3	$55	$315
103	$10.00	$5.00	20	$5	$320
104	$5.00	$10.00	21	$5	$325
105	$10.00	$5.00	36	($5)	$320
106	$15.00	$5.00	30	($10)	$310
107	$30.00	$5.00	33	$25	$335
108	$5.00	$10.00	0	($15)	$320
109	$10.00	$15.00	34	$5	$325
110	$15.00	$5.00	3	($10)	$315
111	$30.00	$5.00	21	($25)	$290
112	$60.00	$5.00	18	($55)	$235
113	$120.00	$5.00	5	($115)	$120
114	$240.00	$5.00	24	$235	$355
115	$5.00	$10.00	22	($5)	$350
116	$5.00	$15.00	22	($10)	$340
117	$5.00	$30.00	7	$25	$365
118	$10.00	$5.00	0	($15)	$350
119	$15.00	$10.00	20	$5	$355
120	$5.00	$15.00	31	($10)	$345
121	$5.00	$30.00	21	$25	$370
122	$10.00	$5.00	12	($5)	$365
123	$15.00	$5.00	33	$10	$375
124	$5.00	$10.00	35	($5)	$370
125	$5.00	$15.00	26	($10)	$360
126	$5.00	$30.00	3	$25	$385
127	$10.00	$5.00	15	$5	$390
128	$5.00	$10.00	0 0	($15)	$375
129	$10.00	$15.00	30	$5	$380
130	$15.00	$5.00	24	$10	$390
131	$5.00	$10.00	20	($5)	$385

132	$5.00	$15.00	22	($10)	$375
133	$5.00	$30.00	25	$25	$400
134	$10.00	$5.00	31	$5	$405
135	$5.00	$10.00	2	($5)	$400
136	$5.00	$15.00	0	($20)	$380
137	$10.00	$30.00	36	$20	$400
138	$15.00	$5.00	22	$10	$410
139	$5.00	$10.00	28	($5)	$405
140	$5.00	$15.00	1	$10	$415
141	$10.00	$5.00	10	$5	$420
142	$5.00	$10.00	6	($5)	$415
143	$5.00	$15.00	15	($10)	$405
144	$5.00	$30.00	27	$25	$430
145	$10.00	$5.00	25	($5)	$425
146	$15.00	$5.00	3	($10)	$415
147	$30.00	$5.00	0 0	($35)	$380
148	$60.00	$10.00	11	$50	$430
149	$5.00	$15.00	34	$10	$440
150	$10.00	$5.00	21	($5)	$435

PROFIT DURING SESSION (SPINS 1-150)

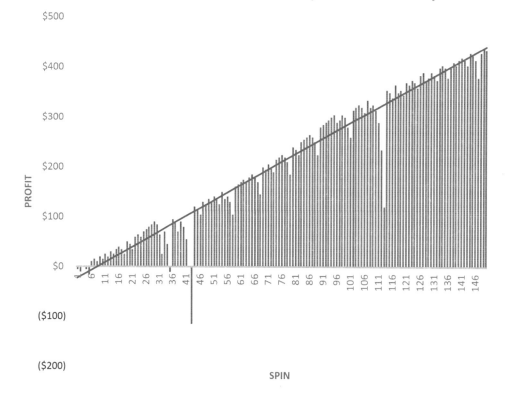

	Example 8: The Keefer Roulette System (Continued)				
Spin	Player 1's Bet (Black)	Player 2's Bet (Red)	Outcome	Profit/Loss	Balance
151	$15.00	$5.00	0	($20)	$415
152	$30.00	$10.00	30	($20)	$395
153	$60.00	$5.00	11	$55	$450
154	$5.00	$10.00	20	($5)	$445
155	$5.00	$15.00	32	$10	$455
156	$10.00	$5.00	24	$5	$460
157	$5.00	$10.00	13	($5)	$455
158	$5.00	$15.00	7	$10	$465
159	$10.00	$5.00	24	$5	$470
160	$5.00	$10.00	22	($5)	$465
161	$5.00	$15.00	12	$10	$475
162	$10.00	$5.00	26	$5	$480
163	$5.00	$10.00	19	$5	$485
164	$10.00	$5.00	36	($5)	$480
165	$15.00	$5.00	5	($10)	$470
166	$30.00	$5.00	29	$25	$495
167	$5.00	$10.00	14	$5	$500
168	$10.00	$5.00	23	($5)	$495
169	$15.00	$5.00	17	$10	$505
170	$5.00	$10.00	35	($5)	$500
171	$5.00	$15.00	15	($10)	$490
172	$5.00	$30.00	22	($25)	$465
173	$5.00	$60.00	13	($55)	$410
174	$5.00	$120.00	18	$115	$525
175	$10.00	$5.00	1	($5)	$520
176	$15.00	$5.00	32	($10)	$510
177	$30.00	$5.00	0 0	($35)	$475
178	$60.00	$10.00	10	$50	$525
179	$5.00	$15.00	15	($10)	$515
180	$5.00	$30.00	9	$25	$540
181	$10.00	$5.00	17	$5	$545

182	$5.00	$10.00	33	($5)	$540
183	$5.00	$15.00	21	$10	$550
184	$10.00	$5.00	7	($5)	$545
185	$15.00	$5.00	20	$10	$555
186	$5.00	$10.00	28	($5)	$550
187	$5.00	$15.00	9	$10	$560
188	$10.00	$5.00	32	($5)	$555
189	$15.00	$5.00	21	($10)	$545
190	$30.00	$5.00	25	($25)	$520
191	$60.00	$5.00	33	$55	$575
192	$5.00	$10.00	31	($5)	$570
193	$5.00	$15.00	24	($10)	$560
194	$5.00	$30.00	22	($25)	$535
195	$5.00	$60.00	19	$55	$590
196	$10.00	$5.00	5	($5)	$585
197	$15.00	$5.00	36	($10)	$575
198	$30.00	$5.00	32	($25)	$550
199	$60.00	$5.00	18	($55)	$495
200	$120.00	$5.00	15	$115	$610

PROFIT DURING SESSION (SPINS 1-200)

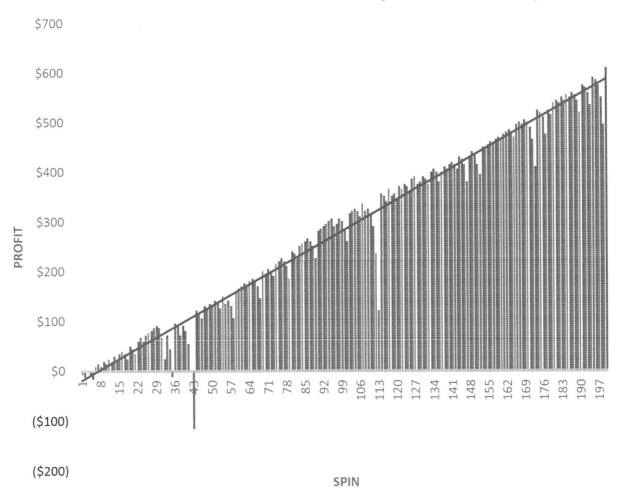

As we discussed in the previous chapter, there are times where you will lose at roulette while using the Keefer Roulette System. Although scarce, I wanted to also show what a losing session looks like. This table was an actual losing session I encountered, in which I lost $1,600 over the course of 88 spins. After losing the ninth consecutive bet, it was time to quit for the day.

Example 9: The Keefer Roulette System

Spin	Player 1's Bet (Even)	Player 2's Bet (Odd)	Outcome	Profit/Loss	Balance
1	$5	-	Odd	($5)	($5)
2	$10	$5	Zero	($15)	($20)
3	$15	$10	Odd	($5)	($25)
4	$30	$5	Odd	($25)	($50)
5	$60	$5	Even	$55	$5
6	$5	$10	Odd	$5	$10
7	$10	$5	Even	$5	$15
8	$5	$10	Even	($5)	$10
9	$5	$15	Even	($10)	$0
10	$5	$30	Even	($25)	($25)
11	$5	$60	Odd	$55	$30
12	$10	$5	Even	$5	$35
13	$5	$10	Odd	$5	$40
14	$10	$5	Odd	($5)	$35
15	$15	$5	Odd	($10)	$25
16	$30	$5	Even	$25	$50
17	$5	$10	Odd	$5	$55
18	$10	$5	Even	$5	$60
19	$5	$10	Even	($5)	$55
20	$5	$15	Even	($10)	$45
21	$5	$30	Odd	$25	$70
22	$10	$5	Even	$5	$75
23	$5	$10	Odd	$5	$80
24	$10	$5	Even	$5	$85
25	$5	$10	Even	($5)	$80
26	$5	$15	Even	($10)	$70
27	$5	$30	Even	($25)	$45
28	$5	$60	Even	($55)	($10)
29	$5	$120	Even	($115)	($125)
30	$5	$240	Even	($235)	($360)
31	$5	$480	Odd	$475	$115
32	$10	$5	Odd	($5)	$110

33	$15	$5	Odd	($10)	$100
34	$30	$5	Even	$25	$125
35	$5	$10	Even	($5)	$120
36	$5	$15	Odd	$10	$130
37	$10	$5	Odd	($5)	$125
38	$15	$5	Odd	($10)	$115
39	$30	$5	Even	$25	$140
40	$5	$10	Zero	($15)	$125
41	$10	$15	Even	($5)	$120
42	$5	$30	Even	($25)	$95
43	$5	$60	Odd	$55	$150
44	$10	$5	Even	$5	$155
45	$5	$10	Odd	$5	$160
46	$10	$5	Odd	($5)	$155
47	$15	$5	Even	$10	$165
48	$5	$10	Odd	$5	$170
49	$10	$5	Even	$5	$175
50	$5	$10	Odd	$5	$180
51	$10	$5	Odd	($5)	$175
52	$15	$5	Even	$10	$185
53	$5	$10	Odd	$5	$190
54	$10	$5	Odd	($5)	$185
55	$15	$5	Even	$10	$195
56	$5	$10	Even	($5)	$190
57	$5	$15	Even	($10)	$180
58	$5	$30	Odd	$25	$205
59	$10	$5	Odd	($5)	$200
60	$15	$5	Even	$10	$210
61	$5	$10	Even	($5)	$205
62	$5	$15	Odd	$10	$215
63	$10	$5	Odd	($5)	$210
64	$15	$5	Odd	($10)	$200
65	$30	$5	Even	$25	$225
66	$5	$10	Even	($5)	$220
67	$5	$15	Odd	$10	$230

68	$10	$5	Odd	($5)	$225
69	$15	$5	Even	$10	$235
70	$5	$10	Odd	$5	$240
71	$10	$5	Even	$5	$245
72	$5	$10	Odd	$5	$250
73	$10	$5	Even	$5	$255
74	$5	$10	Odd	$5	$260
75	$10	$5	Odd	($5)	$255
76	$15	$5	Even	$10	$265
77	$5	$10	Even	($5)	$260
78	$5	$15	Even	($10)	$250
79	$5	$30	Odd	$25	$275
80	$10	$5	Even	$5	$280
81	$5	$10	Even	($5)	$275
82	$5	$15	Even	($10)	$265
83	$5	$30	Even	($25)	$240
84	$5	$60	Even	($55)	$185
85	$5	$120	Even	($115)	$70
86	$5	$240	Zero	($245)	($175)
87	$10	$480	Even	($470)	($645)
88	$5	$960	Even	($955)	($1,600)

PROFIT DURING SESSION (SPINS 1-88)

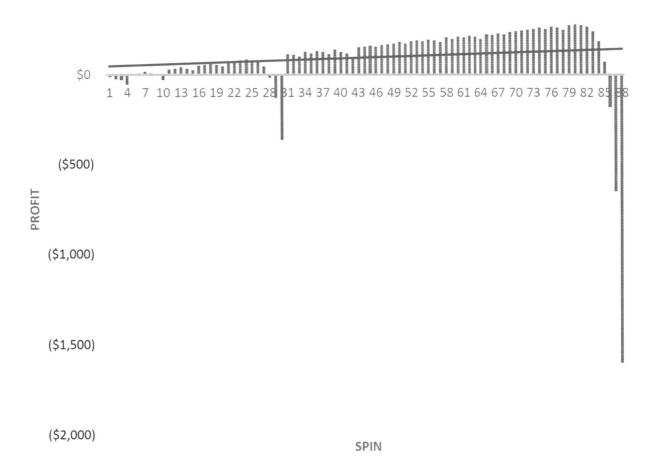

Notes: As you can see from the chart, after 80 spins (approximately 1 hour 45 minutes of play), we were up $280. Had we stopped there, it would have been another winning session, with an average earnings per hour of over $150 and an average earnings per spin of $3.50. Unfortunately, we had no idea the next eight spins would lead to a Streak of 9.

CHAPTER 5

CHOOSING THE RIGHT GAME

While the Keefer Roulette System does greatly increase your profits over time, players are still responsible for choosing the right game. Some games offer more spins per hour, others may appear to be more random, and some wheels may produce several streaks. Selecting the right table may be the difference between making $75 per hour and $125 per hour. It may also be the difference between winning $400 and losing $1,000.

Today, there are several options of roulette games—live tables as you would find in your local casino, electronic or digital games also found in casinos, and online games. Let's take a look at the pros and cons of each type.

Live Tables

Pros

- Tend to be very random

- Strictly regulated by gaming commissions

- Allow players to watch the actual ball spin around and land on the wheel

- More social and exciting

Cons

- Typically a bit slower, depending on the dealer

- Other players can also join the table, slowing down payouts and gameplay

- Some dealers subconsciously start many spins in the same area of the wheel and may have several results from the same area of the wheel

Electronic Tables

Pros

- Some electronic tables use an actual wheel and ball, spun automatically so players can still watch the ball spin and land on the wheel

- Bets are placed digitally, cutting down on betting time and payout time

- Typically average between 40 and 45 spins per hour so can be quicker than some live tables

- One player can run the system by himself, although he will have to bring enough money for two players and will have to keep track of bet sizes for each side and record each result (this can become complicated)

Cons

- Some may be less random due to spin speed and starting the spin in the same spot at times

- Not found at every casino

- Often, these tables have limited seating

Online Casinos

Pros

- There are several online options

- Players can play online anytime, from the comfort of their homes

- Players do not have to worry about other players joining and slowing gameplay

- Very fast-paced so several spins per hour

- One player can run the system by himself

Cons

- Only legal to play in certain states

- Difficult to know how random the program is as each spin is the result of a Random Number Generator (RNG) algorithm

- Typically takes much longer to withdraw profits into your bank account

- While two players can use an online casino, they may sometimes have to use the same computer screen to make the bets as the opposing wagers must be done on the same table/spins

My preference for using the Keefer Roulette System is to have my team play at a live casino. I prefer to go really late at night or very early in the morning on weekdays as an empty table can often be found. Playing at a live table gives you the most control and allows you to watch the dealer, the spinning wheel, and the ball landing in the slot. It helps to have a dealer who is quick at spinning the ball and paying winning bets. The nice thing about my system is that when a team can find an empty table, the partners only need a few seconds to place their two bets prior to each spin. Once the spin is over, the dealer only has one bet to swipe and one bet to pay and all payouts are 1:1 so it should only take a few seconds for this as well. With this being said, an empty table and quick dealer could potentially result in 50+ spins per hour. At that rate, the team should expect a profit of over $150 per hour!

Lastly, when choosing the right table, ensure the table stakes are appropriate. If each player brought $960, you will need to find a table with a $5 minimum bet. You must also ensure the table maximum allows nine increasing bets based on the betting chart from earlier in this book. For the table to work properly, a $5 min table must also carry a $1,000 max bet. Anything less than that will not allow you to make a $960 bet should you lose eight spins in a row.

CHAPTER 6

BANKROLL MANAGEMENT AND KNOWING WHEN TO QUIT

The final chapter of this book stresses one more key element of succeeding with the Keefer Roulette System—managing your bankroll. Although it may seem elementary, without properly managing your bankroll, you will be unable to utilize my system to make thousands of dollars. If you stick to a few simple rules, your bankroll will continue to grow steadily.

The first rule of bankroll management is to only play with what you can afford to lose. Yes, this system is highly probable in earning you a return most of the time. However, there will be occasions where you will lose money in a session. When first starting to use the Keefer Roulette System, it is important that you and your partner build up enough capital for at least a couple losing sessions. If you will be starting at a $5 table, you will each need $960 per session to give yourselves the best odds of winning. Prior to your first session, you should each have a separate gambling fund of at least $1,920 (enough for two sessions) set aside for roulette. This money should not be your rent or mortgage payment, grocery money, or kids' tuition. In fact, it should be money that will not alter or negatively affect your current life in any way. Using only funds that are set aside for gambling activities will allow you to think more clearly when playing roulette. Those who play beyond their means and use money that is critical to everyday life might stray from the betting pattern. This type of gambler makes poor decisions in regard to table selection, betting, and risk management.

One key that has helped me to be successful with my system is maintaining a totally separate bank account, just for seed money and profits from using the Keefer Roulette System. Whenever I go play roulette, I simply take out the required funds for the day and once I have a nice profit, I return my initial investment plus the profit. If you do this as well, it will keep you from overextending yourself and give you a great way to watch your initial investment grow over time. Rather than watching a stock or mutual fund price chart, simply checking the balance of this separate account will be evidence of your returns.

Many people who read this book will keep their jobs and make money with my system on the side. This is a great option as your roulette account can then become a retirement or savings account, used later in life or in an emergency. Others may use this account to put an additional $500 toward their mortgages each month or to enroll their children into private schools. You may even want to use your profits from this system to fund other investments, such as real estate or a business.

Some people may even use this system to provide for their families as it may produce a higher income than working a day-to-day job. In this case, only a certain predetermined amount should be withdrawn for personal use on a weekly or monthly basis so the account does not get too low to re-invest. Whatever your goals are with this system, staying balanced and in control of your roulette funds will be paramount.

Another important aspect to bankroll management is to *always have a gameplan going into each session.* This means going in with a plan to play for one hour or to play 100 spins then quit. If you plan on playing all day, you may want to take a break every so often to refresh your batteries and refuel. In my experiences, going in with a gameplan is the best way to cut down on losing sessions. Typically, I will sit down knowing I will be playing for 100 spins or two hours, whichever comes first. After the session, I either leave for the day with extra cash in my pocket, go grab a bite to eat or do something unrelated to roulette, or find another open table and start my next 100-spin session.

After using my system and building your roulette bankroll, you and your partner may decide to go up in table stakes. Instead of betting $5 to start, perhaps you will start with $10 as your first unit. Of course, you must find a table that will support both a $10 starting bet and a $1,920 bet (required after losing eight straight spins when starting with $10.) When you do this, be sure to have enough funds in your account to fund at least three sessions. If you lose a session at higher stakes, you may have to return to your initial stakes until the account is built back up. Never over-extend the funds in your roulette account!

The final point I have in regards to bankroll management is to keep detailed records of everything. Each live session I play is recorded in a small ledger that I carry with me. This ledger contains each spin of the session and the result of each spin. I then put my sessions into a database for further analysis. This helps to determine the individual and overall success of my sessions. On top of that, I also maintain a spreadsheet detailing the following: Session Date; # of Spins; Time Played; Profit/Loss; Profit Per Spin; Profit Per Hour; and Total Profit—a running balance of what my system has netted me since my first session. Doing these simple things will be very beneficial long-term.

In addition to sound bankroll management principles, players must also know when to quit a session. My first rule about knowing when to quit is that when a team reaches a Streak of 9, or nine consecutive spins where one player loses each time, the team cannot play another session until the next day. If you happen to lose nine straight spins, the table may be unbalanced/ unfair, the dealer may not be optimal, or perhaps you just ended up at a very unlucky table. Either way, avoid these tables—stretching your luck is not recommended.

Another sign that I look for at tables are streaks of less than nine. For example, if you are at a table and over the first thirty minutes there are several streaks of four, five, or six spins where one teammate loses each spin, that is probably not a good table to continue with. Remember, the most profitable tables you can find are extremely random. In fact, because of how the betting pattern is designed in the Keefer Roulette System, if a table never has a streak of three or more, your team will average very close to $5 profit per spin. Back-and-forth streaks are the only things that lower your average profit per spin. Many spins of Zero and double-Zero are also not good indicators. Always try to find the most random table possible.

Another key time to quit a session will be determined by your gameplan. If you start a session with the intent of playing 100 spins, try to cash out as close to that mark as possible. If you decide to play for two hours, play for two hours. As long as your plan going in is founded on reasonable expectations, you will be wise to follow that as an exit strategy as well.

Finally, if you are at a live table at a casino and other players join the table, it may present a good opportunity for you to quit. Some players will come in and not know all the rules of the game. These players take longer to place bets, collect winnings, and make decisions. Other players may make several bets all across the board and slow the gameplay drastically. Also, if there are a number of players at the table betting different amounts on the same wagers, it may take more time for inexperienced dealers to process payouts on each spin. Keep in mind that the more spins your team sees per hour, the more money you will make so anything that will decrease the number of spins will also decrease your profits.

SOURCES

1. "Martingale (probability theory)." Wikipedia. 5 December 2014. Internet (http://en.wikipedia.org/wiki/Martingale_(probability_theory)). 12 December 2014.

2. "Martingale Variations - Types of Popular Betting System." Roulette Systems Info. 2014. Internet (http://roulettesystemsinfo.com/martingale-variations.htm). 12 December 2014.

Printed in the United States
By Bookmasters